Edmund Hillary – climbing
He liked boxing, but climbing became his great love at the age of 16 and Hillary, a New Zealander, gained lasting fame in 1953 when, with Sherpa Tenzing Norgay, he conquered Everest. Many had tried but none had reached the summit of the world's highest mountain before. Hillary died in 2008, aged 87

Gordon Bennett – sponsorship
The millionaire American newspaper owner, who died in 1918, was one of the first great sport sponsors. He also behaved like a modern superstar, getting drunk and behaving so badly that the phrase 'Gordon Bennett!' (meaning 'I don't believe it!') became popular. He sponsored sailing and motor contests, as well as a hot air balloon race that still exists

Muhammad Ali – boxing
Voted the BBC's sportsman of the century in 1999, Ali – who changed his name from Cassius Clay in 1964 – is widely regarded as the best heavyweight boxer of all time and is known as 'The Greatest'. The American, born in 1942, campaigned for racial equality, refused to fight in the Vietnam War, and is one of the iconic figures of the 1960s

Henry VIII – multi-sports
Henry was a brilliant rider from the age of three and spent a third of his life on horseback despite his size – 9 inches taller than average, and not thin. Outstanding at archery, fencing and hunting, and good at ... and bowls, he

THE WHAT ON EARTH? WALLBOOK
TIMELINE
OF SPORT

2008 – Frenchman Francis Joyon smashes Ellen MacArthur's round-the-world sailing record by two weeks, finishing in 57 days

2005 – Ellen MacArthur sails single-handed round the world in a record time of 71 days

2005 – Steve Fossett makes the first non-stop circumnavigation of the globe in an aircraft. It takes 67 hours. Fossett went missing in September 2007 whilst flying over the Nevada desert. His body has never been found

Filipino ... as the best boxer in history, beats Antonio Margarito to become the only man ever to win world titles at eight different weights

2005 – Californian Danny Way ju... the Great Wall of China on a skat... – the first person to clear the Wa... without motorised help

2002 – Miki Ando, from Japan, is the first woman to land a quadruple Salchow – four rotations in one jump

1999 – The Breitling Orbiter 3 – piloted by Bertrand Piccard (Switzerland) and Brian Jones (GB) – completes the first non-stop, round-the-world flight by a hot air balloon in just under 20 days

1997 – Mike Tyson bites Evander Holyfield's ears – both of them – during a world title fight and is disqualified and banned from boxing

1997 – Briton Andy Green drives Thrust, a jet-propelled car that looks like an aeroplane, through the sound barrier across the Nevada desert. It sets a world land speed record of 763mph

1994 – Former US champi... Tonya Harding is banned ... life from ice skating after ... part in an attempt to brea... the leg of Nancy Kerrigan, one of her rivals

1992 – Mike Tyson is convicted of rape and jailed. He serves three years

1986 – Frank Mundus, who inspired the main shark-hunting character in the film *Jaws*, sets a world record for a fish caught with rod and reel. He lands a great white shark weighing 3,427lbs – the same as 14 heavyweight boxers

1986 – A 20-year-old Mike Tyson beats Trevor Berbick – the last man to fight Muhammad Ali before Ali's retirement – to become the youngest ever heavyweight champion

1985 – Barry McGuigan wins featherweight boxing final against Eusebio Pedroza

1984 – Torvill and Dean skate to 'Bolero' and win Olympic gold in Sarajevo with nine perfect sixes

1978 – Ken Warby, an Australian speedboat racer, sets a water speed record of 317mph in his self-built boat, *Spirit of Australia*

1978 – Welshman Leighton Rees wins the first ever world darts championship

1978 – Muhammad Ali beats Leon Spinks, winning the world title for a record third time

1969 – Robin Knox-Johnston sails single-handed and non-stop around the world, starting and finishing in Falmouth, Cornwall. He takes 312 days

1967 – Muhammad Ali refuses to fight in America's war against Vietnam: *'I am not going 10,000 miles to murder, kill and burn other people simply to help continue the domination of white slave-masters over dark people the world over...'* He is convicted of draft evasion, stripped of his titles and banned from boxing until 1970

1964 – Cassius Clay, a former Olympic champion from the US, converts to Islam and changes his name to Muhammad Ali. He becomes the most famous boxer ever – and the BBC's sportsman of the century

1967 – Francis Chichester becomes the first person to sail single-handed around the world via the 'clipper' route. It takes nine months and one day

1963 – Henry Cooper floors Cassius Clay (Muhammad Ali), but loses

1968 – Al Oerter... American discus... is the first athlet... gold at four suc... Games

1953 – New Zealander Edmund Hillary and Sherpa Tenzing Norgay are the first climbers to reach the top of Everest, the world's highest mountain

1927 – The first big sponsored darts tournament, the *News of the World* championship, starts in Britain

1924 – George Mallory and Andrew Irvine disappear on an attempt to climb Mount Everest. Do the British pair reach the summit before falling on their descent?

1908 – Leeds publican Foot Anakin plays darts in court to challenge the law that bans the game from pubs. Anakin throws three 20s and the court clerk cannot match it – so magistrates decide it's a game of skill and end the ban

1908 – Jack Johnson, from Texas, is the first black world heavyweight champion, defeating Tommy Burns in Australia – enraging many white supremacists in the US

1909 – Ulrich Salchow, a Swedish skater, is the first to make a jump on the ice in competition. He wins the world title ten times

1906 – Gordon Bennett starts a 'who can fly the farthest' hot air balloon race, the Gordon Bennett Trophy. It is still going today

1898 – Joshua Slocum sails into Newport, Rhode Island – the first person to sail solo around the world. It takes him three years

1889 – John L. Sullivan beats Jake Kilrain in the 75th round of a brutal bare-knuckle fight in Mississippi. It is the last heavyweight title fought without gloves

1882 – Kano Jigoro invents judo, a new martial art, at his Kodokan exercise hall in Tokyo

1874 – Florence Crauford Grove (he was a man), a member of the Alpine Club, leads the first ascent of Mount Elbrus in Russia, Europe's highest mountain

1862 – Jacko, a terrier, kills 60 rats in 2 mins 42 secs, an average of 2.7 secs per rat. Ratting is a popular entertainment, especially for gamblers in London

1859 – The National Rifle Association is formed in Britain to improve shooting skills (and help the army)

1855 – In Australia, James Kelly and Jack Smith fight for 6 hrs 15 mins – the longest recorded bare-knuckle fight in history

1857 – The Alpine Club is formed in London. Members need to have climbed a mountain of at least 13,000ft

1774 – Sport can be ve... dangerous for players... fighting and cudgel fi... are popular. To win, a ... must 'break' his oppon... head: draw blood that ... at least an inch

1798 – A Turkish sultan, Selim III, shoots an arrow 972 yards – more than half a mile. With the wind behind them, the top Turkish archers could shoot an arrow three-quarters of a mile

1783 – The first flight by humans in a hot air balloon is made in France by the Montgolfier brothers

1520 – Henry VIII ... good wrestler, an... fencer. 'When he ... the ground shake... him,' said a visiti... Venetian noblema...

1620 – Jousting comes to an end owing to the rise of gunpowder

1280 – The longbow of Gwent becomes the new English weapon, requiring hours of enforced practice at butts located safely outside towns

1292 – Tournaments featuring archery, wrestling, riding skills and one-on-one combat often turn into brawls, with many deaths – more than 50 at one event in Germany

1181 – Chrétien de Troyes, a poet and story-teller widely renowned as 'the inventor of the modern novel', finishes his work *Lancelot*, telling of the knight's great deeds as a jouster

1320 – A German expert, believed to be named Liutger, writes a manual, with drawings, on the art of fencing. It is one of the world's oldest surviving sports books, and is now kept at the Royal Armouries Museum in Leeds

1200 – Cock... was the 'ent... sport and th... was Shrove ... when blood... schoolchild... off to 'pit' th... against each

AD 700 – Sumo wrestling matches in Japan are held for the first time, on the seventh day of the seventh month, with much music and dancing

AD 420 – Bodhidharma Indian traveller with a f... huge beard, arrives in C... where he becomes a g... teacher in improving th... and body. According to ... Buddhists, he is the fou... the martial arts

AD 399 – Gladiator schools are closed down in the reign of Emperor Honorius, who also bans men from wearing trousers

AD 50 – Fidenae amphitheatre near Rome collapses, killing 20,000 spectators

AD 106 – Trajan lays on 123 days of games, bringing in 11,000 gladiators, to celebrate victory in war against the Dacians

AD 80 – The Colosseum opens in Rome and Emperor Titus declares 100 days of games to celebrate. These include hungry lions chasing and eating criminals

246 BC – The first gladiator fights are held in Rome

186 BC – Lions and panthers are introduced to Roman games, to kill or be killed by 'bestiarii', trained specialists in animal combat

648 BC – Pankration, the most brutal fighting sport in all history – with eye-gouging, kicking and biting allowed – is first won by Lygdamis of Syracuse

500 BC – Olympic superstar Milo of Kroton tries to pull apart a split in a tree trunk, gets his arms stuck, and is eaten by wolves

688 BC – The first Oly... boxing match is won ... Onomastos of Smyrna

Nadia Comăneci – gymnastics
Millions of girls fell in love with gymnastics after the stupendous performances of Olga Korbut in the 1972 Olympics and, in Montreal four years later, the Romanian Nadia Comăneci. Aged just 14, she scored the first perfect 10 mark in Olympic history, and had six more 10s on the way to winning three gold medals. She won two more in 1980

Pierre de Coubertin – Olympics
The wealthy Frenchman was responsible for the Olympic Games as we know them, having first thought of the idea of reviving the ancient Olympics in 1889. It took a while: the first modern Games were held in Athens in 1896. De Coubertin studied education in Europe and America, and was a great believer in the benefits of playing sport

Roger Bannister – athletics
He didn't run on a track until he was 17 – and seven years later he gained world fame as the first man to break the four-minute barrier for the mile. Bannister, an Oxford student, was spurred on by failure in the 1500m in the 1952 Olympics. He trained harder, and ran the famous 3 min 59.4 sec mile in May 1954

Gaius Diocles – chariot racing
Move over Tiger Woods and David Beckham – Gaius was the biggest-earning sportsman of all time, according to research in the US. He won nearly 1,500 chariot races before retiring aged 42, and was cheered on by crowds of 250,000 at Rome's Circus Maximus. His prize money of 36 million sesterces would have fed the city of Rome for a year

MEN'S & WOMEN'S ATHLETICS WORLD-RECORD HOLDERS

Year	Name	Event	
2014	RENAUD LAVILLENIE (FRA)	POLE VAULT	
2013	WILSON KIPSANG (KEN)	MARATHON	2H
2011	BETTY HEIDLER (GER)	HAMMER	
2009	DAVID RUDISHA (KEN)	800M	1M
2009	USAIN BOLT (JAM)	100M	
2009	USAIN BOLT (JAM)	200M	
2008	YELENA ISINBAYEVA (RUS)	POLE VAULT	
2008	DAYRON ROBLES (CUB)	110M HDLS	
2008	TIRUNESH DIBABA (ETH)	5000M	14M
2008	GULNARA SAMITOVA-GALKINA (RUS)	3000M ST-C	8M
2005	BARBORA SPOTAKOVA (CZE)	JAVELIN	
2005	KENENISA BEKELE (ETH)	10,000M	26M
2004	KENENISA BEKELE (ETH)	5000M	12M
2004	SAIF SAAEED SHAHEEN (QAT)	3000M ST-C	7M
2003	PAULA RADCLIFFE (GB)	MARATHON	2H 1
2003	YULIYA PECHONKINA (RUS)	400M HDLS	
1999	MICHAEL JOHNSON (USA)	400M	
1998	HICHAM EL GUERROUJ (MOR)	1500M	
1996	JAN ZELEZNY (CZE)	JAVELIN	9
1995	INESSA KRAVETS (UKR)	TRIPLE JUMP	
1995	JONATHAN EDWARDS (GB)	TRIPLE JUMP	
1993	QU YUNXIA (CHN)	1500M	3M
1993	WANG JUNXIA (CHN)	10,000M	29M
1993	JAVIER SOTOMAYOR (CUB)	HIGH JUMP	
1992	KEVIN YOUNG (USA)	400M HDLS	
1991	MIKE POWELL (USA)	LONG JUMP	
1990	RANDY BARNES (USA)	SHOT-PUT	
1988	YORDANKA DONKOVA (BUL)	100M HDLS	
1988	FLORENCE G-JOYNER (USA)	100M	
1988	FLORENCE G-JOYNER (USA)	200M	
1988	GALINA CHISTYAKOVA (USSR)	LONG JUMP	
1988	GABRIELE REINSCH (E GERM)	DISCUS	7
1987	STEFKA KOSTADINOVA (BUL)	HIGH JUMP	
1987	NATALYA LISOVSKAYA (USSR)	SHOT-PUT	
1986	JÜRGEN SCHULT (E GERM)	DISCUS	7
1986	YURIY SEDYKH (USSR)	HAMMER	8
1985	MARITA KOCH (E GERM)	400M	
1983	JARMILA KRATOCHVÍLOVÁ (CZE)	800M	1M

Timeline events

2004 – Hossein Rezazadeh – 'The Iranian Hercules' – sets an Olympic weightlifting record of 263.5kg, roughly the weight of five jockeys

2008 – Usain Bolt of Jamaica sets a 100m world record of 9.69 secs at the Beijing Olympics – and reaches the fastest running speed ever recorded by a human, 27.278mph, in the 60-70m stretch

2013 – Oscar Pistorius, the South African 'Blade Runner' who has no legs and runs on springy artificial limbs, is sent to jail after shooting his girlfriend Reeva Steenkamp

2005 – Yiannis Kouros, a Greek-Australian ultra runner, runs 643 miles in a six-day race and sets four of his 154 world records. His feet swell from size 9 to size 11 in a six-day race

2003 – Paula Radcliffe, one of Britain's most popular athletes, sets a world record of 2 hrs 15 mins 25 secs in the London Marathon. The men's record is more than 11 minutes faster

1997 – Carl Lewis retires after winning 17 Olympic and World Championship gold medals in sprinting and long jump

1991 – American long jumper Mike Powell leaps 8.95m to beat, by 5cm, Bob Beamon's world record that has stood since the 1968 Olympics

1990 – American Randy Barnes sets a world shot-put record. He was later banned for taking drugs

1988 – Olympic 100m-champion Ben Johnson, from Canada, is disqualified for taking steroids and sent home from Seoul in disgrace

1983 – Jarmila Kratochvílová, of Czechoslovakia, sets the longest-standing world record in athletics, running the 800m in 1 min 52.28 secs. No woman has come close to it in the last ten years

1981 – Coe/Ovett/Coe/Ovett/Coe: the holders of the world mile record between 1979 and 1981. When Britain's Steve Ovett and Seb Coe, great middle-distance rivals, were at their peak, they were constantly setting records

1981 – The London Marathon is born – and it becomes the biggest annual fundraising event in the world, with 36,500 entrants

1976 – Japan, led by the brilliant multiple champion Sawao Kato, win the men's team gymnastics gold at the Olympics – for the fifth time in succession

1976 – Fourteen-year-old Romanian gymnast Nadia Comăneci is the first to be given a perfect 10 by Olympic judges

1984 – Men are throwing the javelin so far that it's dangerous, so officials change the rules on javelin design so that it doesn't travel such a distance

1968 – American Jim Hines is the first athlete to break the 10-second barrier at 100 metres – his world record of 9.95 secs stands for 15 years

1964 – Dick Fosbury gains fame for his new style in the high jump, going over the bar backwards in a move known as the 'Fosbury Flop'. Now all jumpers use it

1960 – Wilma Rudolph, 'the fastest woman in the world', wins three Olympic golds for the US in Rome

1958 – Larisa Latynina, a great Russian gymnast, wins the world title aged 29, while pregnant

1954 – Roger Bannister runs a mile in 3 mins 59.4 secs at Oxford, gaining world fame as the first man in the world to go below four minutes

1949 – Adi Dassler, a Bavarian shoe maker, starts a company called Adidas that will become a household name. His brother Rudi formed Puma

1948 – Dutch athlete Fanny Blankers-Koen – 30-year-old mother of two – wins four gold medals in the 1948 Olympics (100m, 200m, 80m hurdles, sprint relay)

1946 – Sixteen paraplegics compete in the first Stoke Mandeville wheelchair games

1936 – American athlete Jesse Owens wins four Olympic gold medals at the Berlin Olympics and is snubbed by Hitler for not being Aryan and by the American president for being black

1936 – Stanisława Walasiewicz from Poland finishes second in the Olympic 100m final. She later changed her name to Stella Walsh and when she died in 1980, doctors discovered she was really a man

1924 – Britain's Eric Liddell wins the Olympic 400m in a record time of 47.6 secs – a new world record

1920 – Tug-of-war makes its last of five appearances as an Olympic sport, and Britain's team (all policemen) win gold

1920 – A Fre... swim-run-cy... race called ... Trois Sports ... for the first ... the original ... of triathlon. 1974 before ... first modern triathlon wa... in the US

1912 – The two-handed javelin is an Olympic sport for the one and only time. Athletes had to throw with right and left arm and add the scores together

1908 – Dorando Pietri collapses yards from the marathon finish and is helped over the line, but is disqualified

1904 – Fred Lorz finishes first in the Olympic marathon in St Louis, but is disqualified because he was driven in a car for 11 of the 26 miles

1896 – Baron Pierre de Coubertin forms the International Olympic Committee in Paris. Eleven countries support his plan to stage the first modern Olympics in Athens

1895 – Spiked running shoes are invented by Joseph William Foster, a shoemaker from Bolton. His shoes are worn in the 1924 Olympics, and his company eventually becomes Reebok

1891 – The first recorded water ballet takes place in Berlin – and later becomes synchronised swimming

1878 – Madame Anderson, a great pedestrienne (long-distance walker) from London, walks a quarter of a mile every quarter-hour for 28 days, barely sleeping in that time, in an arena in Brooklyn

1875 – Jackson Haines, a ballet dancer who became the founder of modern figure skating, dies of tuberculosis aged only 35. He invented modern ice skates

1868 – The New York Athletic Club is formed by a group of Irish-Americans. They refuse to admit black and Jewish members for 100 years, leading to a boycott in 1968

1867 – A freezing January day brings hundreds of skaters on to the ice in a lake in Regents Park, London. The ice breaks and 40 drown

1809 – Thousands of people watch on Newmarket Heath as the famous Captain Robert Barclay completes an amazing feat for a bet – walking 1,000 miles in 1,000 hours, one mile per hour. That's seven weeks without a night's sleep. His feet look like lumps of raw meat at the end

1797 – The Gymnasticon, a strange looking contraption, is the world's first gym exercise machine, invented by Englishman Francis Lowndes to help people exercise their joints and muscles

1792 – A famous 58-year-old pedestrian from Yorkshire, Foster Powell, walks from York to London and back in less than six days – nearly 70 miles a day

1789 – Pedestrianism – walking races, and walking long distances for bets – becomes very popular. Donald Macleod, a great Scottish soldier and fencer, walks 1,680 miles from Inverness to London, back again, and to London again, at the age of 100. He made the final journey to check why his pension had not been paid

1526 – A bear called 'The Poet' escapes its chains in a ring in London and bites the head off a spectator

500 – Olympia is looted by Visigoths, Avars, Vandals, Slavs and Turks

393 – Theodosius I suspends the Olympics as pagan ritual

267 – Olympia is sacked by the Heruli, a tribe from southern Russia

490 BC – Legend has it that Pheidippides, a Greek messenger, dies of exhaustion after running 25 miles to Athens from Marathon with news of a great victory

582-573 BC – Three Greek events similar to the Olympics are born: the Pythian, Nemean and Isthmian Games are held regularly at Delphi, Nemea and Corinth

708 BC – Oxylos, founder of the province where Olympia is situated...

776 BC – Koroibos of Elis, a local cook/ritual sacrificer, wins a 100-pace running race across a field to Zeus's altar, called the Stade (hence 'stadium'). He is the first Olympic champion

1700 BC – Bull-leaping is a ritualistic sport undertaken by men and women in Bronze Age Crete

Olympics hailed as a triumph

BY OUR ANCIENT GREECE EDITOR,
Olympia, 776 BC

Baker can barely contain his joy after winning the known world's most prestigious race

AT AN ANCIENT sanctuary in one of Greece's most far-flung corners a historic race took place yesterday between athletes from across the known world.

The contest was held at Olympia, a religious site dedicated to the ruler of the Greek gods, Zeus, by the inhabitants of the nearby city of Elis. Athletes were brought together from many different countries by the chance to race against each other and become famous throughout Greece.

These Olympic Games, held every four years, consist of a single race, called the Stade: a 100-pace sprint across a field towards the altar of Zeus. This year's victor, Koroibos, is a local baker from Elis, and he was awarded the customary Olympic prize, a wreath made from olive leaves, a hallowed symbol of his athletic ability.

One of our reporters spoke to Koroibos, who had this to say about his victory:

"I am completely ecstatic to have won! Before the race, I had never been so nervous of anything in my life. The Games are the greatest athletic competition in the world and, looking round at my opponents, I knew I was racing against some of the best athletes. But then the starting trumpet blared and before I knew it I was across the line. The whole crowd was cheering for me and throwing flowers, it was incredible!"

Even though the Stade is currently the only athletic competition at the Games, the whole event lasts many days and includes numerous religious dedications to Zeus. Of these, the most prominent is the ritual sacrifice of a hecatomb, usually a hundred oxen, in the middle of the Games.

The origin of the Games is passionately debated. Many details have been lost to history, sometimes merging into legend and mythology.

One local hero said to have helped establish the Games is Pelops, the same Greek king who gave his name to the large area of southern Greece known as the Peloponnese.

According to folklore Pelops, after expressing his desire to marry the daughter of a local king, defeated her father in a chariot race to prove himself. But, tragically, the king was killed in the race. As a result, athletic events were held in his honour at Olympia in the Peloponnese.

Legend has it that the demi-god Hercules developed the tradition when he arrived at Olympia, holding races in front of the tomb of Pelops. Hercules is also said to have planted the olive tree from which the sacred olive wreaths of victory are made.

More recently, the Games were restarted by Iphitos, a local from Elis. Iphitos says he received a prophecy from the gods that reinstating the Games would provide a time of peace for the Greeks and an opportunity for them to mend their grievances after numerous wars.

However, scouts are known to be interested in the Games for identifying the strongest, fastest athletes. It is believed by some in nearby Sparta that winners and their offspring will make the best soldiers to defend their city in future conflicts.

Game over for chariot champion

BY OUR RACING CORRESPONDENT, Rome, AD 146

Rome's richest and most opulent sporting hero announces his retirement after amazing career

THE CHAMPION charioteer Gaius Diocles, reputed to be the richest sportsman in the history of the world, has announced his retirement at the ripe old age of forty-two. His devoted fans are erecting a monument in the centre of Rome in recognition of his extraordinary achievements, which include victory in nearly 1,500 races.

For someone who began racing at eighteen, Diocles has had an amazingly long and successful run. Competitors put their lives on the line as horses collide, reins become tangled and chariots spin off into the stands. Knives carried in case drivers need to free themselves from their chariots are just as often used as weapons when a challenger pulls alongside.

Diocles is remarkable for surviving so long without being seriously injured. Even his horses have kept out of harm's way – his favourite, Pompeianus, has won two hundred times.

Chariot teams command great loyalty – some fans are even reported to sniff the dung of their favourite racer's horses to check the animals have been eating well. Fights often break out between rival teams before an important race. Fans supporting different teams sometimes hurl nail-studded amulets on to the track at the Circus Maximus, Rome's biggest sports stadium, to 'curse' the opposition.

Diocles' favourite tactic for victory involves hanging back for most of the race, then applying a burst of speed at the last minute when his opponents' horses are tiring.

Diocles is renowned for his lavish lifestyle with as many grand mansions and extravagant feasts as the Emperor himself. It is said that the many millions of sesterces that he has earned in prize money would pay for the upkeep of the entire Roman army for three months.

Lord Eight Deer makes the ultimate sacrifice

MIXTEC RULER, Lord Eight Deer Jaguar Claw, who conquered ninety-four cities during his reign, has died after being sacrificed to the gods. He was known as one of the greatest players of the ball game called ulama, writes our Mesoamerican correspondent in 1115.

Lord Eight Deer was famous for his brutality, having tortured and killed his wife's father and some of his brothers-in-law. But his prowess as a ball-game player is also said to have helped him win over many territories and to become one of the most powerful rulers in Mesoamerica.

Ball games, traditionally played with a rubber ball, are frequently used for conflict resolution, so that the gods can decide which people are winners and which are losers.

Royal panic as King falls

After a two-hour blackout, His Majesty recovers from a jousting accident, but worries linger about a major injury to his leg

BY OUR ROYAL EDITOR, London, 25 January 1536

PANIC SHOOK the nation yesterday when King Henry VIII was knocked unconscious after falling from his horse in Greenwich. Rumours spread that the King was close to death but he finally came round after two hours, although doctors say he has sustained a major injury to his leg.

King Henry, who is mad keen on sport, was taking part in a jousting tournament at Greenwich Palace when the accident occurred. Serious injuries and even death are common in jousting and concerns about King Henry's refusal to give up the sport, even though he is now forty-four years old, are often heard in hushed conversations at the Royal Court.

The King has always devoted a great deal of his time to sporting pursuits. Hunting is perhaps his favourite sport – he often spends five hours a day on horseback hunting deer, and has created many Royal Parks for this purpose. But he is also a proponent of other sports such as 'real tennis' and has built courts at a number of his palaces, as well as a state-of-the-art racetrack at Cobham, in Surrey.

As a young man, King Henry was known for his athletic physique, his great height and his sporting achievements, particularly his skill with a bow and also with a sword. However, yesterday's accident will only lend support to the

arguments of those who worry that Henry's love of sport is increasingly putting his own life, and therefore the stability of the nation, at risk.

Jousting involves two riders galloping at full speed towards each other with the aim of pushing the opponent off their horse using a long lance. The blow that King Henry received yesterday knocked over his horse which fell on top of him.

King Henry has had accidents while jousting before. Most famously in 1524 an opponent's lance hit him just above the eye after he forgot to lower his visor. Miraculously, he walked away entirely unhurt.

Following yesterday's fall, the King's friends and courtiers will be entreating him to stay away from the jousting fields and stick to tennis instead.

Greek wins marathon in revived Olympic Games

BY OUR OLYMPICS EDITOR,
Athens, 11 April 1896

"CHEERS WENT UP such as have never been heard before!" With these words the French nobleman Baron Pierre de Coubertin yesterday celebrated Greece's victory at his revival of the Olympic Games in Athens.

Not since AD 393, when the Roman emperor Theodosius abolished the ancient games as a 'pagan ritual', have amateur athletes pitted themselves against each other in the Olympian spirit. Now, more than 1,500 years on, the ritual has been reborn, with 241 athletes from fourteen nations competing under the scorching sun in forty-three separate events.

The Greek runner Spiridon Louis ran into the Panathinaiko Stadium at the end of a new event called the marathon, inspired by the legend of the messenger Pheidippides who is said to have run twenty-five miles from the town of Marathon to Athens in 490 BC to announce a great victory in battle. But then, after saying "We have won", he died on the spot from exhaustion.

Following his triumph Mr Louis, a water carrier from Marousi, near Athens, has become a national hero. Members of the Royal Family were among the first to congratulate him. Crown Prince Constantine and Prince George ran on to the track to accompany him across the finish line, while King George rose from his seat to applaud. More than 100,000 spectators were in or just outside the stadium, the biggest crowd at any event of these Olympics.

Mr Louis has since been showered with jewellery and given 2,000lbs of chocolate. One fan even offered him his daughter's hand in marriage. But Mr Louis, twenty-four, who already has a wife and two children, politely refused all but a donkey and cart to help him in his water-carrying business.

Greek officials have proposed their country hosts the Games every time they are held. However, Baron de Coubertin is thought to have other plans.

Running cheat hitches lift to finish

THE BIGGEST CHEAT in the history of sport, or just a practical joker? That is the question being asked about Fred Lorz, an American long-distance runner, after yesterday's controversial marathon, *writes our Olympics correspondent from St Louis, Missouri on 31 August 1904.*

After running nine miles, exhaustion forced Mr Lorz to withdraw – so he abandoned the race and took a lift in his manager's car for the next eleven miles to recover.

About five miles from the finish Mr Lorz leaped out of the car and rejoined his fellow athletes, passing the leader Thomas Hicks. After entering the stadium he ran up to the finish line and broke through the winning tape, all the time cheered on by the ecstatic crowds who believed him to be the legitimate winner.

Mr Lorz, who later claimed his stunt was a prank, was quickly disqualified by angry officials while Mr Hicks, who took strychnine sulphate to keep going in the punishing heat, with temperatures soaring to 32°C, was awarded the medal. Only fourteen of the thirty-two race starters reached the finish.

Olympic gymnast with one leg wins gold

TO WIN SIX Olympic medals in a single day is an extraordinary achievement by any standards. But to win them with a wooden leg is no less than a sensation, writes our Olympics reporter from St Louis, Missouri in 1904.

George Eyser, a bookkeeper from St Louis, has had a prosthetic left leg ever since a train ran him over in his youth. But it has not deterred this amazing man, who emigrated from Germany when he was fourteen, from pursuing his passion for sport and competing in this year's Olympiad staged in his home city.

In the first series of events, the turnen exercises that are favoured and promoted by the Germans, Mr Eyser fared poorly. But in the second round of gymnastics, Mr Eyser excelled. He won gold medals in the vault, the parallel bars and the rope climb. Spectators remarked that to have gained enough momentum for the vault while running on a wooden leg was his most remarkable accomplishment.

Mr Eyser relied on his Herculean upper-body strength for the bars and the rope. With arms the size of other men's legs, he took silver medals in the pommel horse and all-round championship, and a bronze in the horizontal bar.

This is the first Olympic Games to introduce the three-tier gold, silver and bronze medal system for first, second and third places – a definite step up from the ancient Games, where victors were merely crowned with a headdress of olive leaves.

Gordon Bennett! Balloon race duo land in the Dales

Intrepid pair battle high-altitude winds, fog and darkness, touching down in Yorkshire field

BY OUR HOME AFFAIRS EDITOR,
Fylingdales, Yorkshire, 2 October 1906

A MANNED GAS balloon made a surprise landing at Fylingdales in Yorkshire yesterday after completing the first ever Gordon Bennett ballooning race. Flying from Paris across the Channel to the north of England in just twenty-two hours, Mr Frank Lahm and Mr Henry Hersey have become the competition's first victors.

Mr Lahm and Mr Hersey were competing against fifteen other balloon teams from seven different countries. Thousands of Parisians turned out at the Tuileries Gardens for the start of the race at 4pm the day before yesterday, to watch the aviators lift off in their remarkable flying machines. There was no set route; it was simply a matter of who could travel farthest in the shortest possible time.

All the balloons were filled with coal gas, a mixture of lighter-than-air elements including hydrogen, which allows them to fly higher and farther than hot air. However, once aloft, they were at the mercy of the wind and all the competitors found themselves heading towards the English Channel. As night fell, Mr Lahm and Mr Hersey decided to risk the sea crossing in their balloon, the *United States*, despite the possibility of landing in the water.

They were guided only by the light of the moon and Mr Hersey's knowledge of high altitude winds from his work at the US Weather Bureau. A dense fog made navigation difficult, but when it evaporated in the morning sun, the pair found themselves flying over the tranquil Berkshire countryside. Continuing north, they eventually landed four hundred miles from the starting point.

The epic race was organised by newspaper magnate James Gordon Bennett Jr, who previously established an automobile racing championship in 1900, and personally won the first transatlantic yacht race in 1866, crossing from New Jersey to the Needles, off the Isle of Wight, in just thirteen days. Mr Bennett is well known for his often eccentric stunts, leading to the popularisation of the phrase "Gordon Bennett!" as an expression of shock.

The new Gordon Bennett balloon race yet again proves the potential of aviation. While these competitors took to the sky in balloons, recent achievements in aircraft by the Wright brothers are causing many to think of flight as a viable way to travel around the world.

Magnificent men in their driving machines

BY OUR MOTORING EDITOR,
Paris, 11 August 1907

THE PEKING to Paris automobile race, which challenged motorists to drive their vehicles 9,317 miles across two continents, has been won by an Italian team in a 40-horsepower Itala.

The automobile, driven by Prince Scipione Borghese of Italy, was besieged by crowds of cheering fans as it crossed the finishing line yesterday.

Borghese's car was by far the most capable of all the entrants, with its large engine. The Italian prince had also scoped out parts of the route on horseback beforehand, widening narrow passages and hiding stores of supplies and fuel along the way.

The race across Mongolia and Siberia was the idea of the French newspaper *Le Matin*, designed more as a test for the fledgling automobile industry than a cut-throat competition. Eleven participants set off from Peking in north-eastern China on 10 June this year in five cars, representing a variety of automobile manufacturers and European nations.

The competitors soon encountered serious obstacles, however, crossing the mountains from China into Mongolia. The Itala team almost ended up in a ravine when the brakes failed going down a steep track. Things did not improve once they reached the vast Gobi Desert. The French team driving the Contal were forced to abandon their vehicle and return on foot. Nearly collapsing from thirst, having used their drinking water supplies to keep the overheating engine cool, they were rescued just in time by local Mongols. Along the way, camels sent out from Peking before the race relayed fuel to the vehicles.

In Siberia the teams had to navigate overgrown and neglected roads and bridges. One such bridge collapsed as the Itala drove over it, almost throwing the vehicle and its occupants into the river below. But in spite of these setbacks, by the time Borghese reached the symbolic Russian border between Europe and Asia on 20 July, he was days ahead of his opponents. By following telegraph lines, the teams have been able to make regular reports of their position and situation, and the latest bulletins show the other teams are still weeks away from Paris.

Many people across the world think that noisy, unreliable automobiles will never replace horses. Borghese's demonstration of the capability and versatility of his Itala may make them think again.

Enemies find peace in football

IN AN EXTRAORDINARY display of humanity, British and German soldiers along the Western Front stepped out from their trenches yesterday to celebrate Christmas together by playing a friendly game of football on an improvised pitch in no-man's-land, *writes our war correspondent from the French front line on 26 December 1914.*

The celebrations stemmed from unofficial ceasefires designed to give exhausted soldiers on both sides a brief respite from deadly conflict over the festive holiday. British troops climbed over into no-man's-land after hearing

carols being sung by their German adversaries. The British offered gifts, food and even Christmas haircuts to the very men who had been shooting at them only hours earlier. In what commentators are describing as one of the most moving moments in the history of warfare, some soldiers used the opportunity to bring back fallen comrades for burial.

Others were reunited with friends and comrades as both sides exchanged prisoners. In unforgettable scenes, thousands of men put down their weapons to celebrate peacefully.

Near Armentières, in northern France, one soldier reported how everyone stopped to watch a game of football that had broken out between enemy teams.

A group of British medics challenged soldiers from Saxony in eastern Germany to one of the most unusual football games in history. Despite the freezing temperatures both teams played a full game across the desolate field in the no-man's-land between the lines of trenches. Ultimately, the Germans got the better of the British, winning 3–2.

Scotsman: Sunday's too special

THE SCOTSMAN Eric Liddell, who withdrew from the 100m because its heats were to be run on a Sunday, has triumphed in the Olympic 400m, writes our Paris correspondent on 12 July 1924.

Mr Liddell, who is the son of missionaries and himself a preacher, would not run on the Sabbath due to his devout religious beliefs. But there were no Sunday races in the 200m, in which he secured the bronze medal, or the 400m, in which he won gold, setting a new world record of 47.6 seconds.

In Mr Liddell's absence the 100m was won by another Briton, Harold Abrahams. (Editor's note: The story of Mr Liddell and Mr Abrahams is told in the Oscar-winning 1981 film, *Chariots of Fire*.)

Titanic win in tennis doubles

BY OUR OLYMPICS EDITOR,
Paris, 22 July 1924

Olympic champion narrowly avoided death on the Titanic after waves washed him to lifeboat

A HEROIC survivor of the *Titanic*, who nearly lost both legs after hours spent in the icy water, has triumphed at the Olympic Games in Paris.

Richard Williams, an American tennis player who was born in Geneva, Switzerland, was travelling first class with his father when the *Titanic* sank on 15 April 1912 after a collision with an iceberg.

As Mr Williams swam away from the ship, the twenty-one-year-old saw

his father being crushed to death by the collapse of its forward funnel. Ironically, the wave caused by the funnel may have saved the young Mr Williams' life, as it washed him towards the safety of a collapsible lifeboat.

On board the rescue ship RMS *Carpathia*, a doctor told him that to guarantee his survival both legs would need to be amputated.

But Mr Williams refused to give in, and after many weeks of daily exercise

he was able to walk, then run and play tennis again.

Mr Williams, already US tennis singles champion in 1914 and 1916 and winner of the Wimbledon men's doubles in 1920, yesterday won a gold medal in the mixed doubles event here in Paris, despite spraining an ankle during the semi-finals. Mr Williams was minded to withdraw, but his partner, Hazel Wightman, would hear none of it and ordered him to play on.

Owens' triumph shows there is no such thing as a master race

BY OUR ATHLETICS EDITOR,
Berlin, 12 August 1936

JESSE OWENS, an American athlete, has won four gold medals here at the Olympics in Berlin, but his runaway success is threatening to turn into a major political incident.

Adolf Hitler, the German Chancellor, under whose ideology those with dark-coloured skin are considered inferior beings, refused to shake hands with the black runner, and was angered to see so many Germans cheering him on. They even pushed autograph books through Mr Owens' bedroom window at the Olympic Village.

It is widely believed that Herr Hitler is attempting to use these Games as a showcase of his belief that those of Aryan (Nordic) descent are physically and mentally superior to other human beings. But the results suggest otherwise. Mr Owens has won the 100m, 200m, 4 x 100m relay and long jump, wearing running shoes made by a German firm owned by Rudolf and Adi Dassler. *(Editor's note: The Dassler brothers later fell out and set up competing companies – Adidas and Puma.)* This is believed to be the first example of sponsorship in an Olympic event for an African-American male athlete.

"Winning the 100m was the most memorable moment," said Mr Owens, who is expected to be welcomed home with a ticker-tape parade when he returns to New York after the Games.

But issues of race are almost as controversial in the US as in Germany. Mr Owens is the grandson of a slave, and racist laws mean that to attend a reception being planned in his honour at the Waldorf-Astoria hotel in New York, he will have to use the service lift – the main lift is only for the use of whites. There are rumours that Mr

Owens may be snubbed by President Roosevelt, who has not announced plans to meet and congratulate the athlete.

Sources close to the German leader have commented on his stance. One adviser said, "Mr Hitler is highly annoyed by the series of triumphs by the marvellous coloured American runner, Jesse Owens. He believes that people whose antecedents came from the jungle are primitive, which explains why their physiques are stronger than those of civilised whites. In his view they should be excluded."

Housewife Fanny crowned 'Queen of Sport'

BY OUR ATHLETICS EDITOR,
Wembley, London, 1948

A DUTCH HOUSEWIFE has won four gold medals at the London Olympics in sensational style. Fanny Blankers-Koen, affectionately known as 'The Flying Housewife', is a mother of two whose success has propelled women's athletics to the top of the Olympic agenda.

Mrs Blankers-Koen, who is thirty, nearly dropped out because she was missing her young children too much. But despite being written off by critics

as "too old to make the grade", and having now raced eleven times in eight days, she has become the undisputed star of the Games.

She won gold medals at 100m, 200m, 80m hurdles and the 4 x 100m relay, in which she made up ground on the home straight to give the Dutch a thrilling win on the line. She also holds the world record in both the high jump and the long jump – but could not, unfortunately, fit those events into her London schedule.

After the Games, Mrs Blankers-Koen returned home to Holland to a rapturous welcome from an enormous

crowd in Amsterdam. She was carried aloft as 'The Queen of Sport' and paraded through the city in a carriage pulled by four white horses.

Later, city officials presented her with a new bicycle so that she could "go through life at a slower pace". Queen Juliana then awarded her a knighthood.

Her achievement matches that of Jesse Owens, who won four golds at the last Games, held twelve long years ago in 1936. Mrs Blankers-Koen, who was just eighteen at the time, also competed in those Games, but she didn't win any medals.

Everest conquered at last

Perilous trek ends in triumph for mountaineering heroes

BY OUR ASIA CORRESPONDENT,
Kathmandu, *30 May 1953*

THE TOWERING PEAK of Mount Everest, at 8,848 metres the world's tallest mountain, was finally conquered yesterday by two courageous men, Edmund Hillary of New Zealand, who took the first step on the summit, and Tenzing Norgay of Nepal. Their epic journey lasted two days, during which they encountered treacherous icefalls and freezing conditions. Everest has long been seen as the biggest remaining challenge in the climbing world, and their achievement places them among the greatest mountaineers in history.

The extreme difficulty of climbing Mount Everest has cost many lives and caused many parties to turn back. An attempt by a Swiss team only last year had to be abandoned just 250 metres from the summit. Mr Hillary and Mr Norgay's ascent proved scarcely less fraught.

Their team – the ninth British expedition – totalled more than four hundred, including 362 porters, twenty Sherpa guides, dozens of supporters and five tons of luggage. After setting up a series of camps, the first team of mountaineers to attempt the summit was forced to turn back after their oxygen equipment failed.

On 28 May the expedition leader John Hunt suggested that Mr Hillary and Mr Norgay make an attempt on the final ascent. After an arduous day's climb they pitched their tent at an astonishing 8,500 metres before turning in for respite from the biting cold. In the morning, Mr Hillary found his boots frozen solid and the men were delayed for two hours. Soon after setting off, they found themselves facing a seemingly insurmountable wall of rock and ice.

"That was the only thing left between us and the summit," said Mr Hillary. "But there was no immediate way to get up on top of it, it looked like the mountain might have defeated us after all. Then I realised I could lever myself up the wall by carefully edging through a crack I had spotted in the ice. Before long, I was hoisting Tenzing up with a rope and we were looking out over the Himalayas," he said.

Spending fifteen minutes on the summit, Mr Hillary left a cross and Mr Norgay some chocolates to mark their achievement. On their descent, they were greeted by another member of the team, Mr George Lowe, bearing a very welcome meal of hot soup.

Olympic Tarzan hits $2m jackpot

JOHNNY WEISSMULLER, the Olympic gold medallist and swimming sensation, has just completed the latest feature film in which he stars as the jungle superhero Tarzan, taking his total earnings past two million dollars, *writes our correspondent from Los Angeles in May 1948.*

Tarzan and the Mermaids is the twelfth film of the *Tarzan* series to star the former champion.

Mr Weissmuller started swimming at the age of nine on the advice of doctors who were treating him for polio. So keen did he become on his treatment that he took a job as a lifeguard, eventually blossoming into one of the greatest swimmers who has ever lived.

Mr Weissmuller won three gold medals at the 1924 Paris Olympics and two at the 1928 Amsterdam Games. Throughout all his Olympic events, he never lost a race.

Swimming the Channel, there and back again!

BY OUR SWIMMING EDITOR,
Dover, Kent, *23 September 1961*

IN AN AMAZING feat of endurance, Argentinian athlete Antonio Abertondo yesterday became the first person to complete a return swim across the English Channel, covering forty-four miles in 43 hours and 10 minutes.

The Channel between England and France is one of the most popular swimming endurance tests in the world. Even the shortest crossing between the two countries involves a gruelling twenty-mile swim from Dover to Calais. Aside from physical fitness, athletes must be able to avoid zigzagging and extending their route while they are buffeted by heavy waves.

Mr Abertondo, who has made the crossing three times in the past, set off on 20 September to make his ambitious round trip. He paused for only four minutes on the French shore before setting off back again. His time was longer than expected, as swimming at night in strong winds made it difficult to keep to the course. With this feat, Mr Abertondo has set a new bar for athletic excellence in swimming.

The Channel crossing has been an established sporting achievement since a ship's captain, Matthew Webb, first completed the swim in 1875, after rough seas had forced him to turn back on a previous attempt. Mr Webb, whose enthusiasm for the sport developed while swimming in the River Severn as a boy, was confronted by an unexpected obstacle – a wandering bloom of jellyfish – but he still made it safely to shore. Sadly, Mr Webb was drowned in 1883 while attempting to cross the Whirlpool Rapids on the Niagara River, just below the famous Niagara Falls that straddle the border between Canada and the United States.

The American swimmer Gertrude Ederle became in 1926 the first woman to swim across the Channel, silencing those who had said a woman would never make it. Known as the 'Queen of the Waves', she made the crossing in only 14 hours and 34 minutes, a record that stood for almost twenty-five years.

Boxing champion put in prison for dodging draft

Legendary fighter defiant as he is sentenced for refusing to sign up: "So I'll go to jail. We've been in jail for four hundred years."

FROM OUR BOXING EDITOR,
New York, 21 June 1967

LEGENDARY BOXER Muhammad Ali was sentenced yesterday for refusing to join the US forces fighting in Vietnam, and is calling upon others to do the same.

The Olympic gold medallist will go to jail for five years and must pay a $10,000 fine for avoiding the call-up. Comparing the Vietcong with black Americans, he said both were struggling against white oppression. Referring to the poor state of black civil rights in the USA, he said, "So I'll go to jail. We've been in jail for four hundred years."

Mr Ali is one of the best known boxers in history, famous for his lively and dynamic fighting style, which he describes in a catchphrase, "float like a butterfly, sting like a bee". He also speaks out about black civil rights and the lowly position occupied by black people in American society and across the world. A deeply religious man,

he changed his name from Cassius Marcellus Clay Jr after joining the Nation of Islam religious group in 1964 and becoming a Muslim.

He began training as a boxer aged twelve, and at eighteen won a gold medal as a light heavyweight in the 1960 Rome Olympics. He caught the public eye again in 1964 when he faced the heavyweight champion Sonny Liston in a now historic fight. Liston was known for a hard-hitting, frenzied style; some suspected him of putting ointment on his gloves to burn his opponents' eyes. Ali managed to keep his cool, dodging Liston's punches and countering with quick jabs, wearing him down until he was declared knocked out after six rounds. After the match, Mr Ali told the press, "I must be the greatest!"

During the fight, Mr Ali also demonstrated his now famous tactic of 'trash talking' – using imaginative insults to rile his opponents. Ali called Liston 'the big ugly bear' and told him he smelled as bad as a bear.

Mr Ali is now awaiting an appeal and intends to use the media spotlight to boost the anti-war movement. He plans to hold talks at universities and Muslim events. As the number of casualties of the Vietnam War continues to rise on both sides, the world's greatest boxer may right now be its most important pacifist.

Best scores a winner for United

THE FOOTBALL legend George Best turned the tide yesterday for Manchester United at the European Cup Final against Benfica, scoring the first of three goals in extra time that won the coveted award for the English team. It is the first time an English team has won the European Championship, *reports our soccer correspondent on 30 May 1968.*

The first half of the match had been inconclusive. Eight minutes into the second half, a header from midfielder Bobby Charlton scored Manchester United their first goal, but the Portuguese team caught up twenty-two minutes later, leaving the score 1–1 at full time.

Only three minutes into the extra time, Best followed up an incredible run with an unexpected dummy move past Benfica goalie José Henrique to tap the ball into the goal. Manchester United consolidated their victory only minutes later, with a goal from nineteen-year-old Brian Kidd, followed by another from Charlton. The final score was 4–1 to Manchester United.

Yesterday's match took place a decade after the plane crash at Munich Airport in 1958 that claimed the lives of many of Manchester United's best players. Charlton, the current captain, and Bill Foulkes, who also played yesterday, were on the plane but escaped to safety.

Best, a winger, is widely considered one of the best players in the world, particularly when playing alongside the other two members of the 'United Trinity', Denis Law and Bobby Charlton.

Nadia makes seven perfect tens

"LADIES AND GENTLEMEN, for the first time in Olympic history, Nadia Comăneci has received the score of a perfect 10." The words of the announcer said it all, writes our Olympics editor from Montreal, Canada in July 1976.

Huge cheers went up for the Romanian gymnast, who is just fourteen, after her stunning performance on the uneven bars. Even though the score could not fit on the board – designed only for decimal numbers up to 9.99, it read 1.00 rather than 10 – the audience knew what had happened and gave Miss Comăneci the standing ovation she deserved.

Then, to everyone's amazement, she achieved this feat six more times, ending the Games with seven perfect 10s, three golds, one silver and one bronze. Miss Comăneci already scored perfect 10s earlier this year at events in the US and Japan, but few believed she could do so at the Olympics, on the biggest stage of all.

Red Rum races to a hat trick

BY OUR RACING EDITOR,
Aintree, 3 April 1977

RECORD-BREAKING horse Red Rum scored another victory yesterday, becoming the first racehorse ever to win the Grand National three times. Despite his age, the twelve-year-old navigated the difficult course at Aintree, on Merseyside, with ease.

Although originally raised as a sprinter for short races of only about a mile in length, Red Rum won his first Grand National in 1973, overtaking the Australian leader Crisp just two strides from the finishing post – setting a new record for the race of 9 minutes 1.9 seconds. A second win the next year cemented Red Rum's reputation as one of the greatest racehorses in history and one of Britain's favourite sports stars.

As a young horse, Red Rum suffered from a disease of the hoof. However, training on the beach and riding through seawater is thought to have helped cure the problem.

Steeplechases require horses to race while leaping over tall fences. At four miles and four furlongs the Grand National is the longest steeplechase event in the UK.

The race, which first caught national attention in 1839, is often described as the greatest test of a horse's ability – tall fences, sharp turns and a water jump at the halfway point cause many competitors to fall.

Yesterday's race also included the first female competitor in the Grand National. Sadly, Charlotte Brew, twenty-one, failed to finish after her horse Barony Fort refused to jump the twenty-sixth fence.

Woman Olympic medal winner was also a man

STELLA WALSH, an Olympic gold medallist who set eighteen world records on the running track, had two names, two nationalities and, it can now be revealed after a tragic shooting in the United States, two genders, *writes our chief sports correspondent from Ohio on 12 December 1980.*

A post-mortem examination carried out on Mrs Walsh, an innocent bystander at an armed robbery in Cleveland, Ohio last week, revealed that she cannot be confirmed a woman, since she had male genitals as well as two pairs of sex chromosomes – one male and one female. Mrs Walsh was, technically speaking, transgender – as much a man as she was a woman.

Mrs Walsh changed her name late in life, having been born Stanislawa Walasiewicz in Poland. She moved to the US in 1911 as an infant, but returned to her native land to compete in athletics events in the late 1920s.

Mrs Walsh moved between the two countries, and in 1932 was offered American citizenship, which would allow her to run for the US in that year's Los Angeles Olympics – however, she changed her mind and decided instead to run for Poland.

During those Games Mrs Walsh won the 100m in a world-record-equalling 11.9 seconds. In 1933 she set two world records in a day, over 60m and 100m, and she won silver in the 100m at the 1936 Berlin Games.

Mrs Walsh was Poland's most popular athlete for many years, setting fifty-one national records, but she returned to the US, finally accepting citizenship in 1947. Briefly married to a boxer, after her retirement from athletics she worked as a sports events organiser.

McEnroe: You cannot be serious!

CONTROVERSIAL TENNIS star John McEnroe yesterday usurped the illustrious title of Wimbledon champion from Björn Borg, ending the Swede's five consecutive years of victory at the tournament, *writes our tennis correspondent from Wimbledon on 5 July 1981.*

Borg started off strongly in yesterday's match, staying comfortably ahead in the first set, but eventually flagged. McEnroe ultimately came out on top, winning the fourth set to become the 1981 Wimbledon champion.

McEnroe and Borg have faced off many times before, and went head to head in last year's Wimbledon final, where Borg was the victor, fuelling a fierce rivalry between the two tennis stars. The pair have been named 'fire and ice' because of McEnroe's famous hot temper and courtside tantrums.

Last week, the American was fined $1,500 for swearing and shouting "you cannot be serious" at the umpire. The phrase, which was heard all over the world on radio and television coverage, has become a popular catchphrase.

Protesters call time out on racist rugby

AN INTERNATIONAL game of rugby was halted yesterday after a pitch invasion by protesters demonstrating against the racist political policies of South Africa. The match was part of a tour of New Zealand by the Springboks, South Africa's white rugby team, *writes our rugby correspondent from New Zealand on 26 July 1981.*

South Africa has followed a set of racial policies known as apartheid since 1948. Racial segregation is enforced by law throughout South African society,

from schools to sport. Its racist regime has inflamed such intense passions that a protest organisation called Halt All Racist Tours has been co-ordinating opposition to the latest tour, although

a rival group, known as Stop Politics in Rugby, has also been formed in a bid to protest against the protesters.

Yesterday's match took place at Rugby Park in Hamilton. The Springbok team were facing Waikato, defenders of New Zealand's most prestigious rugby trophy, the Ranfurly Shield.

After pulling down a fence, hundreds of protesters rushed into the stadium and formed a circle in the middle of the pitch. Police then called the match off.

Underarm Incident: outraged fans insist that it's simply not cricket!

Tactic is "one of the worst things I have ever seen done on a cricket field," says Benaud

BY OUR CRICKET STAFF,
Melbourne, 2 February 1981

AN EXTRAORDINARY row broke out in the cricketing world yesterday as fans booed the Australian team off the pitch, after their last-minute use of underhand tactics brought them victory in the latest one-day match against New Zealand.

Australian bowler Trevor Chappell rolled an unorthodox underarm bowl across the ground to the New Zealand batsman, Brian McKechnie, meaning there was no way he could possibly attempt to score the six runs needed to draw the game. Fans from both sides were unanimous in their disdain for the Australian team's appalling and unsportsmanlike behaviour.

The underarm bowl, which was once common in cricket, was phased out in the nineteenth century and has not seen widespread use since. But while underarm bowling is not currently against the rules in cricket, it is rare and considered bad practice, especially when the umpire is not informed of the bowler's intentions in advance. In this particular case, the bowl was used as a certain and, it seems to cricket fans, dishonest method to prevent New Zealand from attempting a draw.

The infamous bowl – dubbed the Underarm Incident – came at the end of an otherwise thrilling match. New Zealand needed six more runs to tie and there was one bowl remaining. The only way the New Zealand batsman Brian McKechnie might secure a draw was from a high bouncing delivery, off which he could strike the ball high up into the sky for a six.

Just moments before the final bowl of the day, Captain Greg Chappell spoke privately to his younger brother Trevor, telling him to use the underarm tactic. Knowing that it was all but impossible to score a six from an underarm bowl, this would ensure Australia a victory.

As soon as Trevor Chappell rolled the ball on to the cricket field, Mr McKechnie blocked the ball before throwing his bat down in frustration.

Despite this incident handing a victory to Australia for the second time in the final of this series, the team had no chance to celebrate as the crowd booed in disapproval of their tactics. Even the television commentator Ian Chappell, the brother of Greg and Trevor Chappell, was visibly shocked.

Robert Muldoon, the Prime Minister of New Zealand, said it was "the most disgusting incident I can recall in the history of cricket".

Richie Benaud, commentator and former Australian captain, was similarly outraged, describing the Australian team's tactics as "one of the worst things I have ever seen done on a cricket field".

It is thought that yesterday's incident may provoke a revision of the rules.

Johnson admits to being a drugs cheat

BEN JOHNSON, branded the biggest cheat in the history of sport, has finally admitted taking drugs after months of denials and lame excuses.

Mr Johnson, a Canadian sprinter who broke the world record while 'winning' the 100m gold medal at the Olympic Games in Seoul in September last year, has been taking steroids for years, he has revealed to a Canadian government inquiry.

Mr Johnson's doctor revealed that twenty-six days before the Olympics, the runner took a compound of drugs normally used to fatten cattle before they are sent to market. He was sent home from South Korea in disgrace two days after winning, having tested positive for stanozolol, a steroid.

After being disqualified, Mr Johnson lost his medal, his world record of 9.79 seconds was declared invalid, and he was banned from all kinds of competition for two years.

BY OUR CANADA CORRESPONDENT,
Montreal, 13 June 1989

Mr Johnson was inspired throughout his career by his rivalry with Carl Lewis, the great American athlete. Two years ago, when Mr Johnson first broke the world record in Rome, Mr Lewis said, "There are gold medallists at this meet who are on drugs."

Other athletes were also suspicious of Mr Johnson, giving him the nickname 'Benoid' because they were so sure he was on steroids.

After the Seoul Olympics Mr Johnson blamed the doctor who mixed his energy drinks for his drugs test failure, declaring: "I'll pay back whoever did this to me. I never took anything. I have never, ever, knowingly taken illegal drugs."

But, as revealed by his confession to this inquiry, those words were lies. Mr Johnson is also on record as saying, back in 1985, "Drugs are demeaning and despicable. When people are caught they should be thrown out of the sport for good."

Senna dead in tragic crash

Fans mourn as world-famous Brazilian racing driver is killed in controversial Grand Prix

BY OUR MOTOR-RACING EDITOR,
San Marino, 2 May 1994

AYRTON SENNA, the world's most famous racing driver, was killed yesterday in a tragic high-speed crash at the San Marino Grand Prix. The three-times Formula One champion was rushed to hospital in nearby Bologna but died a couple of hours later.

The race did not get off to a smooth start. A collision at the starting line caused several minor injuries in the crowd from flying debris. Competitors had to follow a safety car slowly around the San Marino course for several laps while the track was cleared.

Once the race had properly begun, Senna was in the lead until he came off the track at a sweeping corner during his seventh lap. Travelling at 135mph, he hit a concrete wall to the side of the

racetrack. Pieces of his car littered the tarmac, while aerial shots revealed that he was clearly not moving.

Medical staff quickly pulled him from his vehicle as race organisers waved red flags to signal other drivers to stop. Senna had suffered serious blood loss and head injuries. The duty doctor recommended that he be immediately airlifted to hospital, but even there medical professionals were unable to save him.

Senna had reported previously that the car was handling strangely. Safety concerns were also weighing heavily on his mind after the death of Austrian driver Roland Ratzenburger during Saturday's qualifying sessions.

Murray Walker, the famous veteran BBC motor-racing commentator, said the loss to Formula One was almost impossible to imagine and hard to put into words.

"This is the blackest day for Grand Prix racing that I can remember in the many, many years I have been covering the sport," he said. "For there to be two casualties on successive days is quite appalling – and that arguably one of

them should be that of the greatest driver that has ever lived in the history of Grand Prix racing makes it doubly so."

As one of the most respected names in motor racing, Ayrton Senna will be missed by fans and professionals alike.

Usain Bolt is fastest in history

USAIN BOLT, the Jamaican sprinter, has lived up to all the pre-Games hype by winning three gold medals, all in world-record times, at the Beijing Olympics, *writes our correspondent from China on 23 August 2008.*

The new fastest man on the planet reached a blistering speed of more than 27mph during the second half of the 100m final, nearly a third faster than the famous Jesse Owens in 1936.

Mr Bolt won the 100m in 9.69 seconds, beating his own world record

by 0.03 seconds, taking just forty-one strides from start to finish. According to scientists who have analysed the race, had he not started celebrating before crossing the line he might have run it in 9.55 seconds.

Mr Bolt also won the 200m in 19.30 seconds, beating Michael Johnson's 1996 record by 0.02 seconds, and he ran the third leg of the sprint relay, won by Jamaica in 37.10 seconds, another world best. Now everyone is wondering – can he run even faster in London in 2012?

Olympic champ sent home for kicking ref

AN OLYMPIC GOLD medallist has been sent home from Beijing in disgrace and banned from his sport for life after an extraordinary attack on a referee, *writes our Olympics correspondent from Beijing on 24 August 2008.*

Ángel Valodia Matos, from Cuba – who was a winner at Sydney in 2000 – was disqualified from yesterday's taekwondo bronze medal match for taking too much time over an injury. A furious Mr Matos reacted by pushing the Swedish referee and viciously kicking him in the face, before spitting on the floor.

Tiger takes a break as his career heads for the woods

BY OUR GOLF STAFF,
Palm Beach, Florida, 12 December 2009

GOLFING LEGEND Eldrick Tont 'Tiger' Woods has announced that he is taking a break from the sport after reports of his repeated infidelities have overwhelmed the reputation of the many-times champion. "I need to focus my attention on being a better husband, father, and person," commented Mr Woods yesterday on his website.

Mr Woods and his wife, Elin, have been married for five years. They have two children, a two-year-old daughter and a ten-month-old son.

The announcement was made two weeks after Mr Woods crashed his SUV into a tree outside his neighbour's house in Florida after hitting a fire hydrant. Police gave the golfer a ticket and the

incident was closed, but questions quickly arose about what Mr Woods was really up to on the morning of the collision.

At some point his wife had smashed the window of his car with a golf club. Although at the time she claimed she was rescuing him from the vehicle, allegations have surfaced that he had

cheated on her. "I am deeply aware of the disappointment and hurt that my infidelity has caused to so many people, most of all my wife and children," Mr Woods has since said. "I want to say again to everyone that I am profoundly sorry and that I ask forgiveness. It may not be possible to repair the damage I've done, but I want to do my best to try."

Mr Woods' talent for golf was evident from a young age. He picked up the clubs before he was even two years old. After turning professional in 1996, he went on to win the Masters tournament only a year later in a record-breaking performance, taking home $486,000 in prize money and becoming the first ever non-white golfer to win. Mr Woods has been in the number one spot longer than any other player.

His unique talent and mixed-race background in a predominantly white sport has made Mr Woods an icon to many and he has become one of the most revered figures in sport – admired for his impeccably good behaviour.

As yet there is no indication of how long Mr Woods will take on his career break. Speculation is also mounting that many of his sponsors are now thinking about withdrawing their support.

Armstrong stripped of all honours

BY OUR CYCLING EDITOR,
Austin, Texas, 25 August 2012

CYCLING TITAN Lance Armstrong was yesterday banned from all sports supervised by the US Anti-Doping Agency after revelations about his extensive use of illegal performance-enhancing drugs.

The seven-times Tour de France champion will also be stripped of any titles or awards won after 1 August 1998. Evidence gathered by the US agency shows performance-enhancing drug use or 'doping' has taken place throughout Armstrong's cycling team.

Mr Armstrong, forty, is considered to be one of the greatest cyclists in the world and has repeatedly denied any link between his success and drug use. Yesterday's decision will put his reputation for extraordinary sporting achievement in jeopardy.

He began his sporting career as a triathlete and first cycled professionally in 1992. Overcoming a potentially fatal cancer condition diagnosed in 1996, Mr Armstrong began racing again two years later. Many were inspired by his triumph over the debilitating disease. At the Tour de France, the world's top road cycling competition, he began a record-breaking streak of consecutive wins, taking first place each year from 1999 to 2005. The annual race, which takes place over twenty-three days and is divided into twenty-one stages, is the ultimate test of speed and endurance across punishing routes. Hundreds of cyclists take part every year.

Mr Armstrong has repeatedly been the subject of allegations about doping and in 1999 was found to be using steroids. He then claimed they were an ingredient in medication he used for saddle sores. In the past the American has verbally attacked cyclists

and reporters trying to expose doping, claiming they are obsessed with trying to ruin him and his reputation.

These new allegations combine evidence from a number of different sources, including blood tests, urine samples and even the testimonies of members of his team.

The organisation investigating Mr Armstrong's doping regime called it

"the most sophisticated, professionalised and successful doping program that sport has ever seen". The extent of his cheating, Mr Armstrong's aggressive stance towards those who accuse him, and his status as a man who overcame cancer to become one of the world's greatest athletes, only make the sense of betrayal felt by his fans and fellow sportsmen all the greater.

Blade Runner jailed for five years

Paralympic superstar found guilty of culpable homicide after fatal shooting of his girlfriend

BY OUR SOUTH AFRICA EDITOR,
Johannesburg, 22 October 2014

OSCAR PISTORIUS, the Paralympic athlete, was yesterday sentenced to five years in jail for killing his girlfriend Reeva Steenkamp on Valentine's Day last year. The South African sprinting champion, who is known as the 'Blade Runner' because he runs on specially engineered artificial legs, was taken down from court in Johannesburg to start his sentence. He showed little emotion as he was led away.

Last month, Mr Pistorius was found guilty of culpable homicide – which means that the athlete used excessive force, but in circumstances not amounting to murder – after firing four gunshots into the bathroom door of his house in Pretoria. His girlfriend, who was behind the door at the time, died almost instantly. Mr Pistorius claimed he thought he was being attacked by an intruder.

Yesterday's sentencing ends one of the most sensational stories of heroism and disgrace ever to befall a modern sporting hero.

The life of Oscar Pistorius is now divided into a period of sensational determination and heroism against a disability that threatened to ruin his life – followed by a descent into paranoia and violence, as he became obsessed with guns.

Born without both fibulas (lower leg bones), Mr Pistorius had his legs amputated just below the knee at the age of eleven months. Using a pair of prosthetic legs, his inherent energy began to flow and, encouraged by a teacher at his school, he soon began to take up sports.

After his mother Sheila died when Mr Pistorius was fifteen, his passion for sport became all-consuming. His big breakthrough came in the summer of 2004 when he won the 200m gold medal at the Paralympics in Athens. A star had been born.

Eight years later, at the Olympics in London, Mr Pistorius became the first ever athlete to compete in both the Paralympic and Olympic Games. This double achievement made him an icon in the eyes of the world, showing how with sufficient determination even the most severe physical disability was no

barrier to competing on a level with able-bodied rivals.

Such success also helped transform interest in the Paralympics, bringing new interest from sponsors and spectators, and breaking down the barriers between disabled and non-disabled sports.

But Mr Pistorius' success came at a price. According to friends, personality changes were apparent as early as 2011, when he stormed out of a BBC interview. Sports journalist Graeme Joffe, who co-owned a racehorse with Mr Pistorius, noticed a similar change. "He was showing a spoiled-brat attitude that came out a year later at the Paralympics [in 2012] when he embarrassed the country," he recalled. Mr Joffe was referring to the interview when Mr Pistorius lashed out at fellow Paralympic athlete Alan Oliveira, accusing him of using illegal blades.

In late 2012, Mr Pistorius started dating the South African model Reeva Steenkamp. Just three months later, on 14 February 2013, he shot Miss Steenkamp, claiming that he thought there was an intruder in his bathroom.

His trial began on 3 March 2014, culminating in the sentence that was passed down yesterday. In a statement, the International Paralympic Committee acknowledged that Mr Pistorius had "done a great deal for the Paralympic movement" and would be allowed to compete again, but it is understood his ban will last for at least five years.

Across

1) ___ Ballesteros: famous Spanish sportsman who died in 2011 (4)
4) London guild that opened the first bowling green (7)
6) Pete ___: the most famous baseball player of modern times (4)
8) Teacher from Illinois who invented a new game (8)
9) Greek gets caught in a tight spot (4)
12) Roman emperor who closed gladiator schools (8)
13) W.G. ___: bearded batsman who scores 56,000 runs! (5)
15) Muhammad ___: sporting superhero born Cassius Clay (3)
17) Albert ___: US sports entrepreneur who re-wrote history (8)
19) Traditionally, matches of this sport are held on the seventh day of the seventh month (4)
20) Sports event first held in the exuberant Italian city-state of Venice (7)
22) ___ Rum: a horse who won a grand hat-trick (3)
24) The world's oldest regulated horse race takes place here (9)
25) Animal often carried on the shoulders of a great New Zealand rugby player (5)

26) Queen Elizabeth II and Prince Philip met over a game of ___ (7)
28) A new design makes it travel less far (7)
29) The tyrant who turned his back on black (6)
31) At last! Women's ski jumping was included at the 2014 Winter Olympics in this Russian resort (5)
32) Björn ___: Swede who once had a massive army of female fans (4)
33) World champion with a biting average of 2.7 per second (5)
34) A brilliant swimmer who died in a whirlpool (4)
35) This famous football club was founded over a drink in the Rising ___ (3)

Down

1) Odds are it's a ___ Life (8)
2) Roman ruler who fiddled (4)
3) Meet Danny, the Californian who jumped the Great Wall of China on a ___ (10)
4) Nag mystics rotated about (10)
5) The place where gladiators first fought (4)
7) Cute name for a new sport based on a Michigan engineer's homemade toy (8)

10) Baron de ___: French educationalist who established the modern Olympic movement (9)
11) Item of clothing banned by a Roman ruler (8)
12) The ___: nickname for an Olympic champion who nearly lost a leg in a motorbike crash (10)
14) Jane ___: unlikely author of a book that mentions baseball (6)
16) Tennis star Steffi Graf won a unique Golden ___ (4)
18) Annual sporting festival once played on the ___ Sands (7)
21) Peak fitness is required to mount this one (7)
23) Pierre ___ was responsible for the world's worst ever motor-racing disaster (6)
26) First name of a pair of university students who raced on a river (7)
27) Until 1963, all players were called ___ by their team-mates (3)
30) Acronym for the body that runs the Olympics (1,1,1)
32) Unlikely first name for the man who was one of baseball's greatest (4)

All the correct answers can be found somewhere in this book!

A selection of letters from would-be readers down the ages

He deserves every coin!

I WAS DISTRAUGHT to hear that the great Gaius Diocles is retiring. The new statue being erected in pride of place in Rome will be an enduring testament to his astounding career. Our city has never seen an athlete quite like him.

To all those naysayers who moan that his achievements do not warrant the sackloads of money he has earned, I say "Bah, humbug!" We don't complain about rich planters, politicians and slave owners, so why shouldn't we reward such a superhuman sporting talent who has brought pleasure to millions?

CORNELIUS CARTWRIGHT

Gaius riddance, I say!

GOOD RIDDANCE to Gaius Diocles! The vile sport that has made him so disgustingly rich only promotes violence and chaos. Perhaps now the great chariot racer is gone, the hysteria surrounding the sport will subside.

Chariot racing and gladiator fights are simply a cynical ploy by the authorities to keep the poor and oppressed from demanding their own rights and freedoms. That prize money could be going to building schools, or feeding the hungry. Enough of these celebrity sports stars – what sort of example do they set for the next generation?

DECIMUS DISAPPROVING

Long live the King!

THANK GOD the King is all right! His accident on the jousting field has had the whole country in a worry. Hopefully, it will be a major wake-up call for all those involved with dangerous sports.

In my view, a person's life is far too precious to be thrown away over sport, especially when he holds the stability of the realm in his hands. The King should leave this kind of competition behind and focus on more civilised pursuits.

SALLY SAFELY

Ride on, ride on, Your Majesty!

BEING A GREAT KING means being a leader, a scholar and a warrior.

King Henry demonstrated he has these qualities yesterday on the jousting field. While I was shaken when I read that the King had passed out from his accident, our ruler's athletic ability is inspirational to us all. Please keep jousting, Your Majesty!

JACK JOUST

Marvellous machines

I WAS GRIPPED by your report on motoring enthusiasts and their recent race across the continents from Peking to Paris. The immense distance the vehicles and their drivers travelled is enough to prove the value of this new technology, and may persuade those who say the motor car will never replace the horse to think again.

However, I am just as interested in the new sports it may open up. As these vehicles become faster and more powerful, new exciting races will become a possibility. Bring on the motor car drivers and their marvellous machines!

GARY GASKET

Trains, horses, but not automobiles

THE PEKING TO PARIS automobile race has only demonstrated beyond doubt the failings of these new machines. I don't foresee these noisy, uncomfortable and unreliable contraptions taking off on any significant scale.

Even with the world's greatest equipment and support throughout their journey, we read telegraph reports that the drivers were repeatedly halted by each tiny obstacle they encountered. Travellers should stick to horses and railways – a horse won't run itself off a mountain and you don't have to feed it a supply of diesel to keep it going.

EMILY EQUESTRIAN

The politics of sport

HERE IN NEW ZEALAND, I applaud the strong reaction against the arrival of the Springboks and their national tour. Apartheid is a pernicious, evil ideology, which invades every aspect of a nation's psychology, meaning that the merging of politics and sport is unavoidable.

If the South African government refuses to allow some of our players to compete in their country on account of the colour of their skin, then it is they who are bringing politics and sport together, and we should answer in kind, by taking a firm and unassailable stance against their racist policies.

LARRY LAMB

To comment on any issues in this book – visit www.whatonearthbooks.com/sport

Hey, guys, let's just get on with the game!

I WAS SADDENED to hear about the disruption caused to the rugby game between Waikato and the Springboks.

South Africa is one of New Zealand's favourite opponents and many of us were looking forward to the match.

Politics and sport never mix well. Hijacking sport for the purpose of furthering ideals is a big mistake and detracts from the universal reliability of athletic competition. I hope the tour will continue and this unwelcome episode will come to an end.

ALAN APOLITICAL

CRICKET - 1981

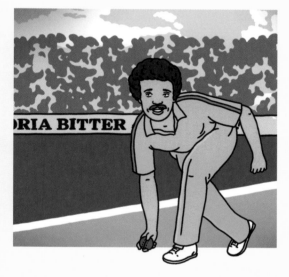

Both underarm and underhand

AUSTRALIA'S BEHAVIOUR yesterday during the final moments of their match against New Zealand was utterly shameful.

How are athletes supposed to keep up a degree of friendly competition when entire matches are decided by such cheap tricks? How are fans supposed to look up to a team so evidently dishonest and unsportsmanlike?

This is not the way cricket was meant to be! Australia's final ploy was immature and insulting to the New Zealand team, which had played incredibly well to recover their position in the match as much as they had.

Australia may have taken home the win, but they gave everyone who witnessed the end of the game a foul taste in their mouth.

Shame on them!

DAVE DISAPPOINTED

Storm in a teacup

I FAIL TO SEE what is so shocking about the Australian underarm bowling incident that is dominating sporting news at the moment. If cricket fans still believe in an idea of 'sportsmanship' they live in a dream world. These are top international competitions.

Australia isn't going to throw away an easy victory over some medieval concept of honour among athletes. They stuck to the rules and won fair and square, so no-one should be blaming them for playing a better game than New Zealand.

REG RULEBOOK

CYCLING - 2012

Sports cheats deserve no sympathy

AS AN AVID follower of Lance Armstrong and his numerous athletic achievements, and a cycling nut myself, I was shocked by the revelations regarding his disgusting doping practices.

All sportsmen need to follow the rules set out for them to ensure there is a level playing field for competition. Doping only gives an athlete an unfair advantage, as well as putting him or her in danger.

What is most disturbing here, however, is Mr Armstrong's repeated denial of allegations against him over the years. Such a dishonest athlete has no place in sport.

The whole incident reminds me of the repeated denials made by Canadian runner Ben Johnson for nearly nine months after the Seoul Olympics in 1988. Cheating has no place in open, fair competition. And what kind of example do these people think they are setting to the younger generation?

TAMMY TRUTH

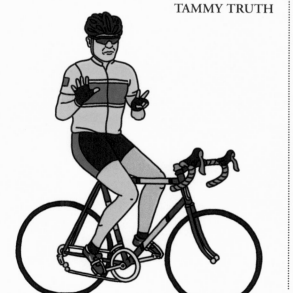

ATHLETICS - 2014

Is sport a proxy for violence?

THE BIG QUESTION which is raised by the whole sorry saga of Oscar Pistorius is to what extent sport provides a peaceful way of venting the violent instincts of people – or does it exacerbate an inherent human inclination to do harm?

Is warfare between and within nations less rife today as a result of our fixation with sport? Or is the opposite true? It's hard to call. Are we as a species more or less violent than our ancient ancestors were, before the era of grandstands and Olympic championships?

Before we rush to judge Mr Pistorius, horrible though his crime was, it may be worth remembering that this man, like other athletes, has been trained all his adult life to compete aggressively in the most challenging situations – this is how to win.

Perhaps most surprising of all about this case is that such tragic accidents do not happen more often in a world that glorifies ruthless competition.

VERITY VIOLENCE

Don't forget the victim's family!

ALL THE FUSS and bother about the trial of Oscar Pistorius just makes me want to weep – no-one seems to remember that the real victims here are the Steenkamp family.

The media hype surrounding this sordid affair must not be allowed to obscure the terrible loss they will suffer for the rest of their lives.

EMILY EMPATHY

See how many of our brain-teasing sports questions you can answer...

RACING (Wheels, Ice & Water)

1. Two Native American swimmers were the first to demonstrate crawl at a race in London. One was called Flying Gull, the other was called:
   a) Chocolate
   b) Tobacco
   c) Sweetcorn
   d) Cotton

2. Which car company did Enzo Ferrari work for before setting up his own car-making company in 1947?
   a) Fiat
   b) Alfa Romeo
   c) Lamborghini
   d) British Leyland

3. Which famous cyclist is nicknamed 'The Cannibal'?
   a) Lance Armstrong
   b) Orlando Borini
   c) Bradley Wiggins
   d) Eddy Merckx

4. What is the fastest speed ever recorded in a motorcycle race?
   a) 157 mph
   b) 184 mph
   c) 211 mph
   d) 217 mph

5. Snowboards were originally known as:
   a) Spords
   b) Smurfs
   c) Snurfs
   d) Snurfers

6. Which Roman emperor cheated his way to glory at the chariot races in AD 67?
   a) Hadrian
   b) Titus
   c) Trajan
   d) Nero

7. Roman charioteer Gaius Diocles is said to have amassed a fortune estimated in modern money to have been worth approximately:
   a) £10 million
   b) £100 million
   c) £1 billion
   d) £10 billion

8. In 46 BC the Circus Maximus in Rome was a chariot-racing stadium estimated to be able to accommodate how many people?
   a) 10,000
   b) 50,000
   c) 150,000
   d) 300,000

9. Where did the the first wheelchair games, the forerunner of the Paralympics, take place?
   a) Milton Keynes
   b) Stoke Mandeville
   c) Stoke-on-Trent
   d) Blackburn

RACING (Legs & Feet)

10. Which of the following horses sensationally won the 2009 Grand National at odds of 100-1?
    a) Red Rum
    b) Mon Mome
    c) Mr Frisk
    d) Shergar

11. The dead body of which famous sporting legend was stuffed and donated to the National History Museum in London:
    a) Mick the Miller
    b) Red Rum
    c) The Darley Arabian
    d) Gordon Bennett

12. Roger Bannister first ran a mile in less than four minutes in which famous city?
    a) London
    b) Paris
    c) Oxford
    d) Cambridge

13. Jarmila Kratochvílová, a Czech runner, has the longest-standing world record in athletics for which event?
    a) 100m
    b) 200m
    c) 800m
    d) 400m hurdles

14. As many as 95 per cent of all racehorses are said to be related to which of the following famous horses?
    a) Lottery
    b) Red Rum
    c) Shergar
    d) The Darley Arabian

15. Gatwick, now London's second-largest airport, was once:
    a) A football ground
    b) A racecourse
    c) A cricket pitch
    d) A motor-racing circuit

16. What caused the 1993 Grand National to be declared a void race?
    a) Riders did not notice there was a false start
    b) A dog ran on to the track
    c) A hailstorm
    d) A bomb scare

17. The first modern Olympic Games were held in which European city?
    a) Athens
    b) London
    c) Paris
    d) Rome

BALL GAMES (Bats, Clubs, Rackets & Sticks)

18. The regulation width for the goalposts in polo is:
    a) 5.2m
    b) 7.3m
    c) 8.4m
    d) 9.7m

19. How many times did Martina Navratilova win the Wimbledon Women's Singles title?
    a) 5
    b) 7
    c) 9
    d) 11

20. Jahangir Khan won 555 straight wins in which sport?
    a) Tennis
    b) Badminton
    c) Squash
    d) Table tennis

21. The longest match in the history of tennis finished with the final set at:
    a) 27–25
    b) 36–34
    c) 62–64
    d) 70–68

22. The first ever international cricket match was held between which two nations?
    a) England and Australia
    b) Australia and India
    c) England and South Africa
    d) United States and Canada

23. Who is supposed to have invented the forerunner to cricket, called stoolball?
    a) Vicars
    b) Merchants
    c) Milkmaids
    d) Blacksmiths

24. Lacrosse was invented by which ancient people?
    a) Aztecs
    b) Romans
    c) North American Indians
    d) Greeks

25. Queen Elizabeth and Prince Philip met over a game of:
    a) Croquet
    b) Tennis
    c) Golf
    d) Badminton

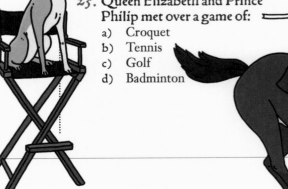

All the correct answers can be found somewhere in this book!

26. What was used for the last time at Wimbledon in 1987?
a) White tennis balls
b) Wooden tennis rackets
c) Chalk tramlines
d) White long johns

27. Alan Shepard is famous for:
a) Rowing across the Atlantic
b) Scoring six sixes in a Test match over
c) Winning four Grand Nationals
d) Hitting a golf ball on the moon

28. Golfer Larry Bruce is the first person known to have:
a) Accidentally eaten his golf ball
b) Scored a hole-in-one on a par 5
c) Killed a pigeon with his tee-shot
d) Fallen head over heels while attempting to play out of a deep bunker

29. What did Jack Nicklaus controversially do on the final hole of the Ryder Cup in 1969?
a) Dance around the green
b) Concede a 2-foot putt to the competition
c) Deliberately sneeze during his opponent's tee-shot
d) Score a hole-in-one

30. What colour jacket is awarded to the winner of the US Masters?
a) Green
b) Blue
c) Red
d) White

31. The American baseball legend Babe Ruth's real first name was:
a) Reg
b) Sid
c) Frank
d) George

BALL GAMES (Hands & Feet)

32. Which Olympic sport did the USA win in every Games between 1936 and 1968?
a) High jump
b) Long jump
c) Ice hockey
d) Basketball

33. Which nickname is given to the Roman girls depicted playing hand-ball on a mosaic in a Sicilian villa?
a) The booby girls
b) The bikini girls
c) The bouncing girls
d) The banana girls

34. The survivors of a plane crash that killed most members of Uruguay's rugby team stayed alive by:
a) Lighting beacons of fire
b) Rowing across the Pacific
c) Drinking their own urine
d) Eating their dead team-mates

35. How did New Zealand rugby player Colin Meads gain his strength:
a) Carrying sheep on his back
b) Wrestling with dingoes
c) Eating copious quantities of spinach
d) Consuming three Shredded Wheat for breakfast each day

36. Which famous sportsman is nicknamed 'His Airness'?
a) Michael Jordan
b) Dick Fosbury
c) Steve Fossett
d) Johan Remen Evensen

37. What was first used in a game of rugby in New Zealand in 1884?
a) A corner flag
b) A rugby ball
c) A whistle
d) A referee

38. In which city was the first Super Bowl championship held?
a) New York
b) Dallas
c) Miami
d) Los Angeles

39. Why did a Danish sports coach invent hand-ball?
a) Because rugby was too violent
b) As a way of improving hand-to-eye coordination skills
c) Because he couldn't walk
d) To prevent windows being smashed by people playing football

40. Michael O'Brien is famous for:
a) Scoring more goals in the World Cup than any other player in history
b) Streaking during a rugby match at Twickenham
c) Founding Chelsea Football Club
d) Establishing the world's first women's football World Cup

41. What punishment was given to boys at Eton who refused to play football at least once a day?
a) Denied dinner
b) Fined and kicked
c) Thrown into a pool of icy water
d) Expelled

42. Footballer Edson Arantes do Nascimento is best known by his nickname:
a) Pelé
b) Maradona
c) Jordon
d) Legendinho

43. Which famous football club was founded in a pub called The Rising Sun?
a) Chelsea
b) Arsenal
c) Sheffield Wednesday
d) Manchester United

SPECIAL SPORTING MOMENTS

44. Ancient Greek Olympic wrestler Milo of Kroton met an untimely death after being:
a) Eaten by wolves
b) Crushed by a tree
c) Struck by lightning
d) Tickled senseless

45. Which country hosted the first ever women's football World Cup?
a) China
b) United States
c) England
d) Germany

46. American sportsman Danny Way is famous for jumping over the Great Wall of China on a:
a) Mountain bike
b) Motorbike
c) Skateboard
d) Pole

47. Ancient Greek athlete Oxylos was banished from his home region near Olympia after:
a) Killing his brother with a discus
b) Getting drunk at the Olympic Games
c) Cheating his way into the running finals
d) Spearing a spectator with a javelin

48. In which sport did a team of British policemen win an Olympic gold medal?
a) Cycling
b) Relay racing
c) Badminton
d) Tug-of-war

49. A Gymnasticon was a primitive type of:
a) Skipping rope
b) Exercise machine
c) Pole vault
d) Jockstrap

50. What technology did Edwin Budding invent in 1830 that revolutionised many sports:
a) Fibreglass
b) Aluminium
c) Pneumatic tyres
d) Lawnmower

Classifieds

THE WALLBOOK CHRONICLE

◆ Our Philosophy

WHO ON EARTH ARE WE?

Here at What on Earth Publishing, we think that learning should always be fun.

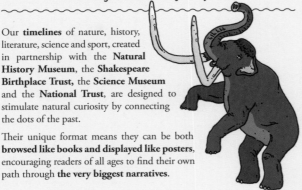

Our **timelines** of nature, history, literature, science and sport, created in partnership with the **Natural History Museum**, the **Shakespeare Birthplace Trust**, the **Science Museum** and the **National Trust**, are designed to stimulate natural curiosity by connecting the dots of the past.

Their unique format means they can be both browsed like books and displayed like posters, encouraging readers of all ages to find their own path through **the very biggest narratives**.

◆ Our Formats

WHAT ON EARTH BOOKS COME IN 3 *Fantastic Formats*

◆ Our *Wallbooks* feature the original two-metre timeline, plus a newspaper packed with stories, pictures, letters, crossword and quiz. Perfect for everyone.

◆ Our *Stickerbooks* each have around a hundred stickers, and a 1.7-metre simplified version of the timeline to fix them on to. Perfect for younger readers.

◆ Our *Posterbooks* are a gigantic three-metre version of the timeline, printed on heavy paper and laminated for extra durability. Perfect for schools.

◆ On Tour

THE AMAZING HISTORY OF THE WORLD IN 20 OBJECTS

COMING TO A VENUE NEAR YOU!
(you merely have to ask)

a BIG BANG of a book!

Find out where it all began. Join **Christopher Lloyd** on the greatest journey of all, the 13.7-billion-year history of the Universe, in his bestselling classic, **What on Earth Happened?**

Now available from Planet Earth's best bookshops.

'Compelling… remarkably far-reaching and even-handed'

THE SUNDAY TIMES

◆ School Visits

The WORLD!! STRANGER THAN FICTION!

We believe that the real world is far more interesting than anything found in fiction. But the fragmented, confined nature of the curriculum can make learning seem all too dry. Our cross-curricular workshops – developed over hundreds of talks at schools, festivals and museums, and available for Year 1 through to Year 13 – are designed to weave narrative threads between different subjects, forge new connections and bring them to life.

'I have been besieged this morning by teachers who have come to say how much their classes had enjoyed the workshops'

Librarian, Hertfordshire

www.whatonearthbooks.com/events

◆ Inset Training

CURIOSITY: antidote to boredom z z z z z

Getting curiosity to flow in the classroom can be a real challenge for teachers working within an established curriculum – yet no-one can learn effectively unless their natural curiosity is engaged. Interweaving neuroscience, memory-based learning techniques and storytelling skills, our **Inset Workshops** are ideal for schools wishing to pursue a more interconnected, curiosity-driven teaching strategy.

'Everyone I spoke to during and after our training yesterday was awe-inspired by the session. It was amazing'

TEACHER, BERKSHIRE

www.whatonearthbooks.com/events

THE WHAT ON EARTH? TIMELINE RANGE
COMPLETE THE SET!

1. Big History **2.** Nature **3.** Sport **4.** Science & Engineering **5.** Shakespeare

Available in **Wallbook**, **Stickerbook** and **Posterbook** formats.

www.whatonearthbooks.com

Written by **Christopher Lloyd**, **Brian Oliver** and **Patrick Skipworth**. Illustrated by **Andy Forshaw**. Designed by **Will Webb**.
Published by What on Earth Publishing Ltd, The Black Barn, Wickhurst Farm, Leigh, Tonbridge, Kent TN11 8PS, United Kingdom.
Printed in China by Waiman. Wallbook is a registered trademark of What on Earth Publishing Ltd. © 2015 All rights reserved.

Contact us at **info@whatonearthbooks.com** or visit our website at **www.whatonearthbooks.com**